Conjunctivitis

Angela Royston

www.heinemann.co.uk

Visit our website to find out more information about **Heinemann Library** books.

To order:

☎ Phone 44 (0) 1865 888066

▤ Send a fax to 44 (0) 1865 314091

💻 Visit the Heinemann Bookshop at www.heinemann.co.uk to browse our catalogue and order online.

First published in Great Britain by Heinemann Library,
Halley Court, Jordan Hill, Oxford OX2 8EJ
a division of Reed Educational and Professional Publishing Ltd.
Heinemann is a registered trademark of Reed Educational & Professional Publishing Ltd.

OXFORD MELBOURNE AUCKLAND JOHANNESBURG BLANTYRE
GABORONE IBADAN PORTSMOUTH (NH) USA CHICAGO

© Reed Educational and Professional Publishing Ltd 2002
The moral right of the proprietor has been asserted.

Designed by David Oakley/Arnos Design
Illustrations by Jeff Edwards
Originated by Dot Gradations
Printed in Hong Kong/China

ISBN 0 431 12858 8 (paperback)   ISBN 0 431 12852 9 (hardback)
06 05 04 03 02   06 05 04 03 02 01
10 9 8 7 6 5 4 3 2 1   10 9 8 7 6 5 4 3 2 1

British Library Cataloguing in Publication Data
Royston, Angela
  Conjunctivitis. – (It's catching)
  1. Conjunctivitis
  I. Title
  617.7'73

Acknowledgements

The Publishers would like to thank the following for permission to reproduce photographs:
Bubbles pp8 (Fran Rombout), 14 (Ian West), 23 (Claire Paxton), Gareth Boden pp20, 24, 25, Martin Soukias pp10, 22, PhotoDisc pp4, 9, 19, 26 (Ryan McVay), Robert Harding p29, Science Photo Library pp5, 7, 12 (Scott Camazine), 13 (Will and Deni McIntyre), 15 (John Durham), 16 (P Marazzi), 17 (St. Bartholomew's Hospital), 18 (Mauro Fermariello), 21 (Mark Clarke), Stone pp11 (Dennis O'Clair), 28 (Robert Daly), Tony Stone (Peter Cade) p27.

Cover photograph reproduced with permission of Science Photo Library.

Every effort has been made to contact copyright holders of any material reproduced in this book. Any omissions will be rectified in subsequent printings if notice is given to the Publisher.

Any words appearing in bold, **like this**, are explained in the glossary.

Contents

What is conjunctivitis? 4

Healthy eyes 6

What causes conjunctivitis? 8

How is conjunctivitis caught? 10

Other causes of conjunctivitis 12

First signs 14

Sticky eyes 16

Treatment 18

Getting better 20

Other treatments 22

Don't spread eye infections 24

Well and healthy 26

Think about it! 28

Answers 30

Glossary 31

Index 32

What is conjunctivitis?

Conjunctivitis is an illness that affects the inside of the eyelid. It can also affect the thin covering of the eye. This book is about conjunctivitis.

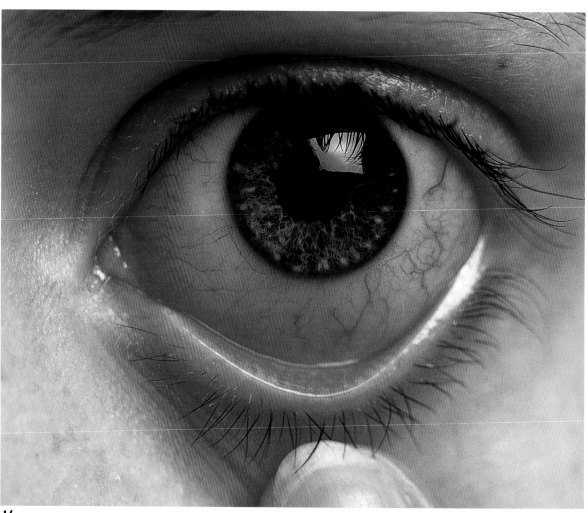

Conjunctivitis is **infectious**. This means it is passed from one person to another.

Healthy eyes

You use your eyes to see. Light enters each eye through the pupil in the centre of the eye.

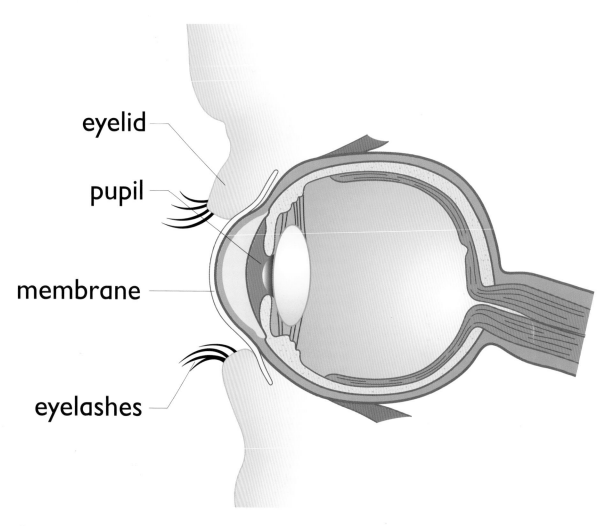

eyelid

pupil

membrane

eyelashes

The eye is covered by a thin skin called a membrane. The membrane stops dirt and **germs** getting into the eye. So do your eyelids and eyelashes.

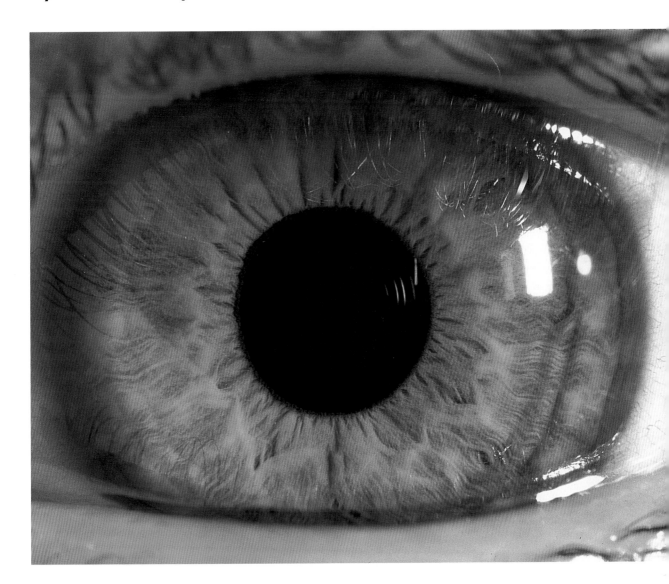

What causes conjunctivitis?

Conjunctivitis is usually caused by **bacteria** or **viruses**. These germs are so tiny you can only see them through a **microscope**.

This photo shows the virus that causes conjunctivitis. It has been **magnified** and coloured so that you can see it more clearly.

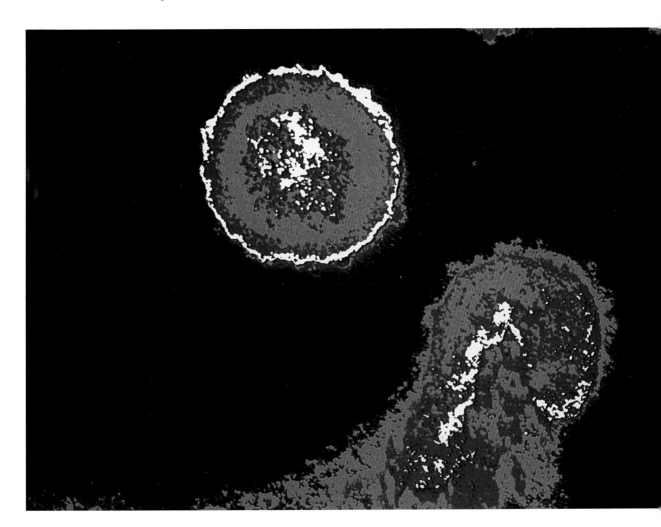

How is conjunctivitis caught?

You catch conjunctivitis when the **bacteria** or **virus** touches your eyes. If a friend has conjunctivitis they might rub some of the **germs** on to their towel.

If you then use the same towel, you may rub the germs into your own eye. Some germs in the swimming pool water may also get into your eyes.

Other causes of conjunctivitis

This photo shows tiny grains of **pollen**, blown from some grass. Pollen causes hay fever and itchy, sore eyes. People who suffer from hay fever or other **allergies** may get conjunctivitis.

Strong **chemicals** can also cause conjunctivitis. The chemicals burn the delicate covering of the eye. People who use strong chemicals should wear goggles to protect their eyes.

First signs

The first sign of conjunctivitis is often an itchy or burning feeling in the eye. Tears help wash dirt and **germs** out of the eye.

When you have conjunctivitis your eye may become a lot more watery than usual. It can also become very red.

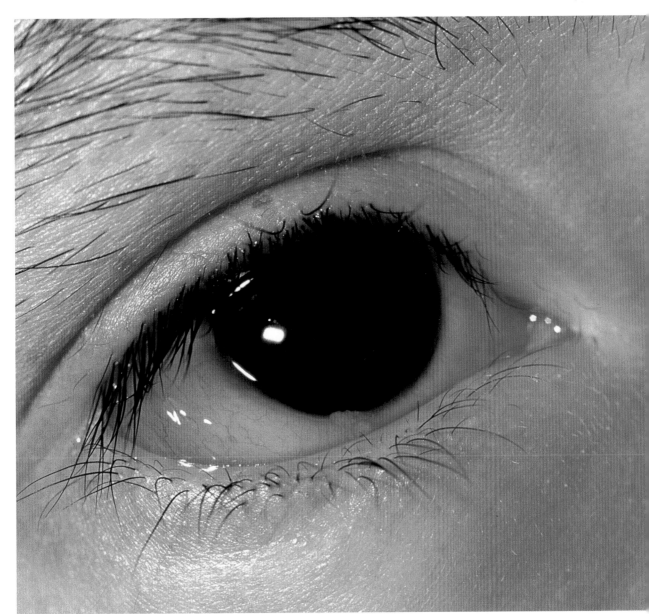

Sticky eyes

As your body fights the conjunctivitis **germs**, it makes a sticky, yellow **pus**. When you are asleep the pus may make your eyelids stick together!

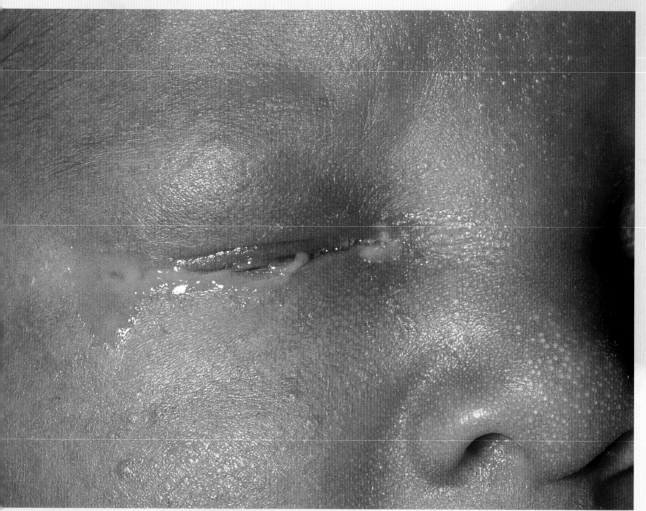

Use cotton wool dabbed in clean, salty water to wipe away the pus. Very bad conjunctivitis is called pink eye because the white part of your eye becomes red.

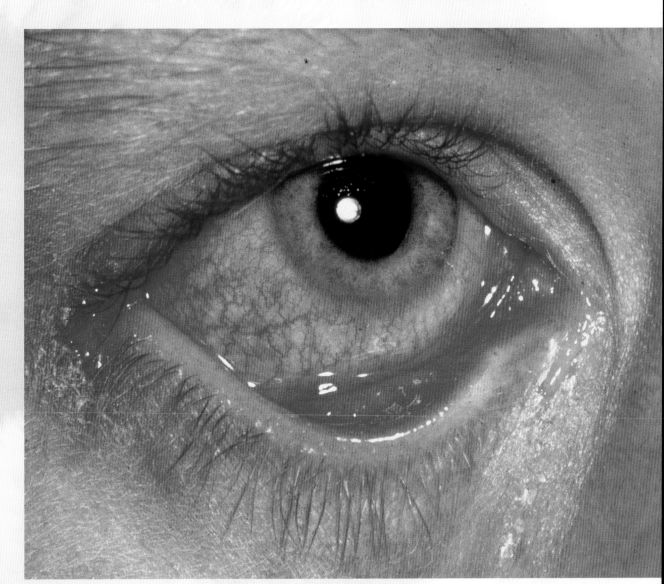

Treatment

If you have conjunctivitis you should have it checked by a doctor. If the illness is caused by a **virus**, you will have to wait for it to get better on its own.

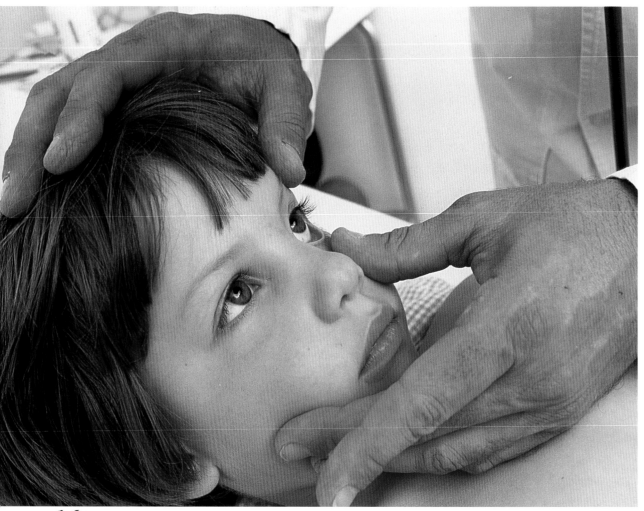

If it is caused by **bacteria**, like this, the doctor will prescribe an **antibiotic ointment**. Antibiotics can kill bacteria, but not viruses.

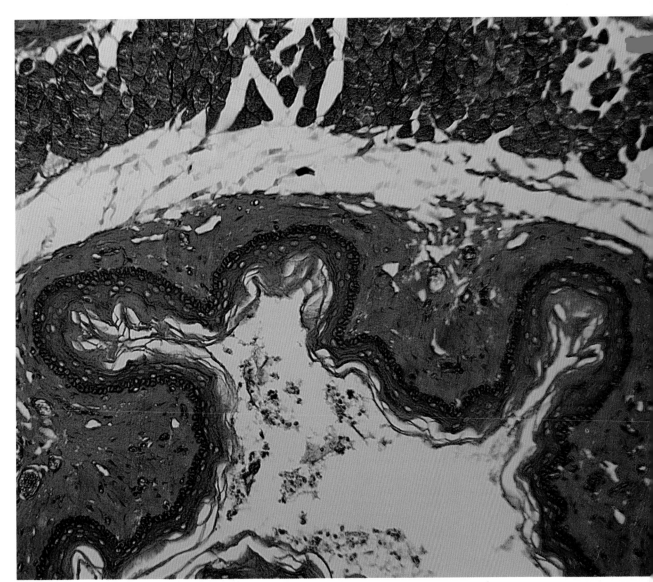

Getting better

The doctor will tell you how often to apply **ointment**. An adult will have to squeeze some ointment into your eye for you.

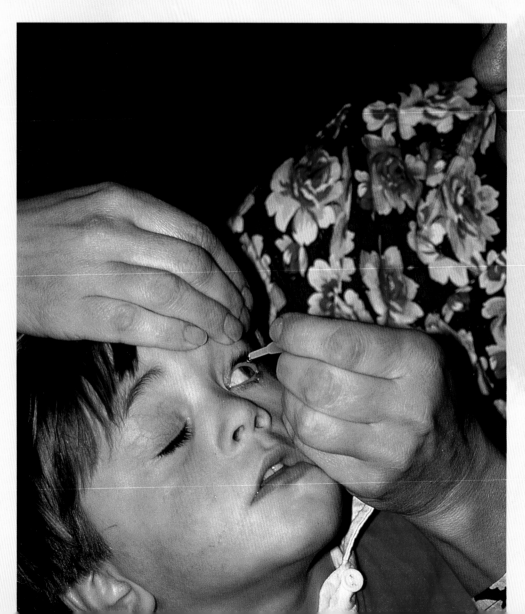

The ointment will start to work after a few days. You must go on using it for as long as the doctor tells you, or your eye may get sore again.

Other treatments

If the conjunctivitis is caused by an **allergy**, a cold **compress** may help. Make a compress using a pad of clean material soaked in cold water.

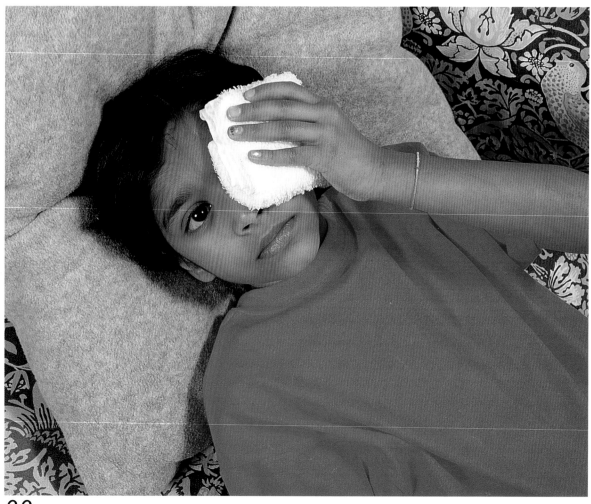

Squeeze out the water and hold the pad over the closed eye. If you get **chemicals** in your eye, bathe it in slightly salty water and see a doctor at once.

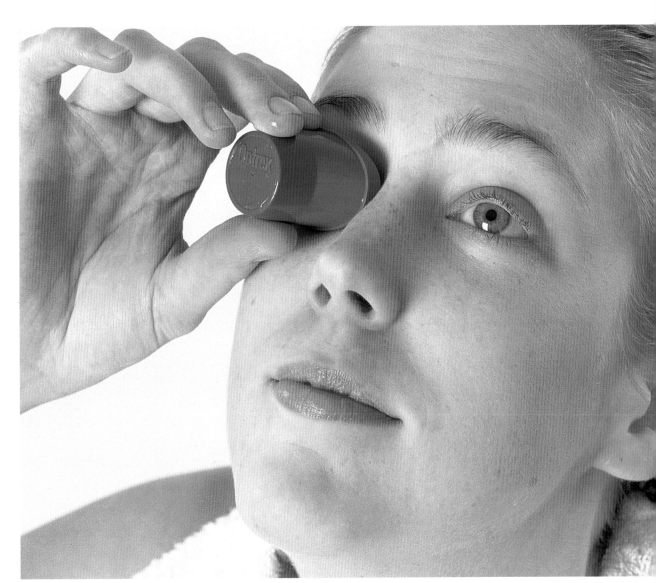

Don't spread eye infections

If you have conjunctivitis or another eye **infection**, try not to pass it on. Don't use towels that other people might use.

Try to avoid catching conjunctivitis. Don't rub your eyes with dirty hands and make sure you keep your hair out of your eyes.

Well and healthy

You are more likely to stay well and healthy if you follow a healthy lifestyle. Take plenty of exercise and try to breathe in fresh, clean air.

Eat good food with lots of fresh fruit and raw vegetables. Wash your face and hands before you go to bed and sleep well!

Think about it!

Sharon has caught conjunctivitis. She was swimming with her friend in the pool. How might Sharon have caught the eye **infection?***

These children wear swimming goggles when they go in the pool. Will goggles stop them catching conjunctivitis?*

*Answers on page 30.

Answers

Page 28

If her friend has conjunctivitis, the **germs** could be carried in the water that splashes Sharon's face. They could also be on the towel that she uses to dry her face.

Page 29

Swimming goggles will help to stop water splashing in their eyes, but some water usually gets under the goggles. Conjunctivitis germs can also still reach their eyes on a towel or their fingers.

Stay healthy and safe!

1 Always tell an adult if you feel ill or think there is something wrong with you.
2 Never take any **medicine** or use any **ointment** or lotion unless it is given to you by an adult you trust.
3 Remember, the best way to stay healthy and safe is to eat good food, to drink plenty of water, to keep clean and to wear the correct clothes.

Glossary

allergy   when something that is harmless to most people causes a part of the body to become sore or itchy

antibiotic   something that kills bacteria

bacteria   tiny living things – most bacteria are harmless but some can make you ill if they get inside your body

chemicals   substances that things are made of

compress   pad of material that has been soaked in a soothing liquid

germs   tiny living things that make you ill if they get inside your body

infection   illness caused by germs

infectious   something, especially an illness, that can be passed from one person to another

magnified   made bigger so that you can see it more clearly

medicine   substance used to treat or prevent an illness

microscope   something that makes very small things look big enough to see them

ointment   oily cream that often contains medicine and is squeezed into the eye or rubbed into the skin

pollen   fine powder made by most flowers and grasses that is blown about and carried by the wind

pus   thick liquid made by the body as it fights germs

virus   tiny things that can make you ill if they get inside your body – viruses are even smaller than bacteria

Index

allergies   12, 22
antibiotics   19

bacteria   8, 10, 19
bathing your eye   23

catching conjunctivitis   10-13, 25, 28-9, 30
chemicals   13, 23
compress   22-3
conjunctivitis   4-5, 8-19, 22, 24-25, 28-30

dirt   7, 14, 25

eyelashes   6, 7
eyelids   4, 6, 7
eyes   4, 6-7, 10-11, 12-13, 14-15, 16-17, 20-21, 23, 25

germs   7, 8, 10-11, 14, 16, 30
goggles   13, 29, 30

hair   25
hay fever   12
healthy life   26-7, 30

infection   5, 28
itchy, red and watery eyes   12, 14-15

membrane   7
microscope   8

ointments   19, 20-21, 30

pink eye   17
pollen   12
pus   16-17

signs of conjunctivitis   14-15
spreading eye infections   24
sticky eyes   16-17
swimming   11, 28-30

towels   10-11, 24, 30
treatments   18-23

viruses   8-10, 18-19